This story is dedicated to my grandchildren: Jonathan Edmon Skaggs, James Logan Skaggs, Mary Charlotte Trammell and Virginia Eudora Trammell.

Misty Monarch Children Illustrators

Takiyah Addie

Melissa Aleman

Jaquez Alford

Sara Banks

William Blessinger

Taylor Bowles

Yekeria Bowles

Aleyah Braham

Reshay Brooks

Keshawn Cameron

Amiaha Clayon

Lindsey Conner

Colton Couch

Rebecca Daniel

Braylan Gates

Wesley Goodrich

Devonte Gordon

Zyterrius Gray

Jhonovon Hall

Matt Heath

Elizabeth Helms

Shamiya Hines

Evian Jaeger

Skyiler Jaeger

Desirae Johnson

Jasmine Kennedy

Korisma Levesque

Adtson Livingston

Kaylee Mcdowell

Vidhi Patel

Molly Perdue

Taylor Porter

DeAndrea Ransom

Precious Signorelli

Tashawn Sinkfield

Logan Skaggs

Nathan Skaggs

Avery Smith

January Stephens

Takiya Terry

Emeryy Thigpen

Mary Trammell

Virginia Trammell

Emary Warrior

Tryist Watts

Addison Worsley

Print information available on the last page

Rev. date: 03/20/2017

To order additional copies of this book, contact:
Xlibris
1-888-795-4274
www.Xlibris.com
Orders@Xlibris.com

Meet Misty Monarch.
Monarch is a kind of butterfly.

2

Monarchs fly north from Florida and Mexico across many states.

Monarch butterflies fly long, long ways to find good feeding gardens.

Warm sun and trail winds help them get where they are going.
On their journey Misty and monarch friends stopped for water in
Texas. A dog barked and scared Misty away.

When the monarchs reach the state of Georgia there are peach orchards and Monarch garden trails.
People have planted flower gardens just for the monarch butterflies.

Mrs. Rosalind Carter, former president Jimmy Carter's wife, started planting butterfly gardens.
Thank you, Mrs. Carter.

People who love butterflies are planting gardens just for butterflies in Meriwether County, Georgia.

Good rain, sun, and soil are needed for flowers and milkweed plants to grow.

In many places there are no milkweed plants in gardens and no butterflies come.

Monarch butterflies have to have milkweed plants to eat and live.

About July monarchs are expected to arrive in Georgia and then find the beautiful gardens with milkweed in them.

As they travel along Misty Monarch makes new friends.

What a beautiful garden there. It must be one of the Meriwether Monarch Trail gardens. Misty will surely stop here.

No! No!. Do not spray insecticides. Killing other insects can harm butterflies. That is one reason they are endangered.

Misty remembers another habitat problem. Back in Mexico too many trees have been cut, endangering the butterfly habitat.

Milkweed is abundant as Misty eats that and other colorful nectar plants, too. Soon she will lay eggs on the milkweed plants.

Misty and other butterflies lay eggs on plants in this and other gardens.

Here is a beautiful black and yellow caterpillar.

It eats and grows and then spins a cocoon.

Wow! The butterfly is spinning and changing inside the chrysalis or cocoon.

This is part of the life cycle of butterflies.
Ah, out comes the beautiful, new monarch.

Making the long trip south must happen soon before a killing frost comes in Georgia.

Glowing sunshine is still warming the wings of the butterflies and the plants are still blooming, but the monarchs must begin their trip south.

Misty gives a goodbye signal and the long trip south to Florida or Mexico begins. The monarchs will hibernate there for the winter.

Misty hopes to see you again next year. Plant some butterfly gardens with milkweed and bright flowers for her!

Printed in the United States
by Baker & Taylor Publisher Services